DATE DUE

GAYLORD			PRINTED IN U.S.A.

THE MIDDLE EAST

Cultures and Costumes Series:

- The British Isles
- Oceania
- Africa
- The Middle East
- China and Japan
- Native America
- Greece and Turkey
- France
- Spain and Portugal
- Northern Europe
- Italy and Switzerland
- Eastern Europe
- India and Sri Lanka

CULTURES AND COSTUMES: SYMBOLS OF THEIR PERIOD

THE MIDDLE EAST

GERARD CHESHIRE
AND
PAULA HAMMOND

MASON CREST PUBLISHERS

www.masoncrest.com

Mason Crest Publishers Inc.
370 Reed Road
Broomall, PA 19008
(866) MCP-BOOK (toll free)
www.masoncrest.com

First printing 2002

1 2 3 4 5 6 7 8 9 10

Library of Congress Cataloging-in-Publication Data available

ISBN 1-59084-434-3

Printed and bound in Malaysia

Editorial and design by
Amber Books Ltd.
Bradley's Close
74–77 White Lion Street
London N1 9PF

Project Editor: Marie-Claire Muir
Designer: Hawes Design

Picture Credits:
All pictures courtesy of Amber Books Ltd.

ACKNOWLEDGMENT
For authenticating this book, the Publishers would like to thank
Robert L. Humphrey, Jr., Professor Emeritus of Anthropology,
George Washington University, Washington, D.C.

Contents

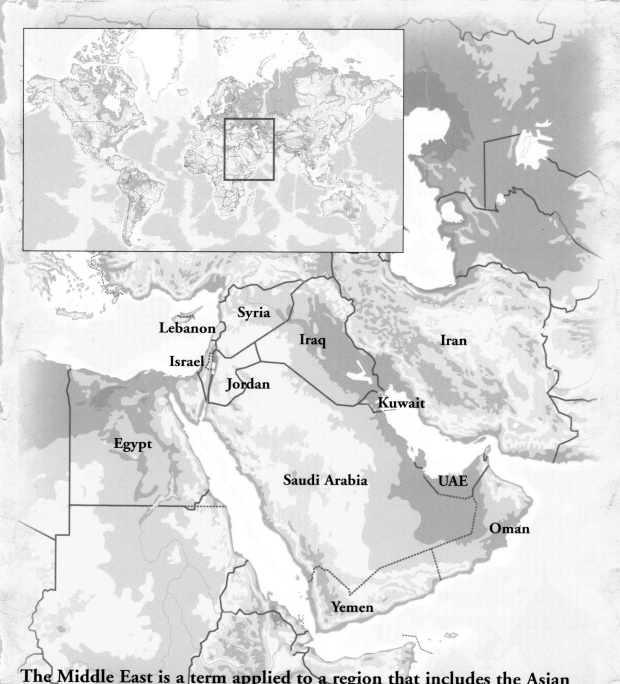

The Middle East is a term applied to a region that includes the Asian part of Turkey, Syria, Israel, Jordan, Iraq, Iran, Lebanon, and the countries of the Arabian peninsula. The term Middle East is also used in a cultural sense for that part of the world predominantly Islamic in culture, in which case the remaining countries of North Africa are included.

Introduction

Nearly every species in the animal kingdom adapts to changes in the environment. To cope with cold weather, the cat adapts by growing a longer coat of fur, the bear hibernates, and birds migrate to a different climatic zone. Only humans use costume and culture—what they have learned through many generations—to adapt to the environment.

The first humans developed their culture by using spears to hunt the bear, knives and scrapers to skin it, and needles and sinew to turn the hide into a warm coat to insulate their hairless bodies. As time went on, the clothes humans wore became an indicator of cultural and individual differences. Some were clearly developed to be more comfortable in the environment, others were designed for decorative, economic, political, and religious reasons.

Ritual costumes can tell us about the deities, ancestors, and civil and military ranking in a society, while other clothing styles can identify local or national identity. Social class, gender, age, economic status, climate, profession, and political persuasion are also reflected in clothing. Anthropologists have even tied changes in the hemline length of women's dresses to periods of cultural stress or relative calm.

In 13 beautifully illustrated volumes, the *Cultures and Costumes: Symbols of their Period* series explores the remarkable variety of costumes found around the world and through different eras. Each book shows how different societies have clothed themselves, revealing a wealth of diverse and sometimes mystifying explanations. Costume can be used as a social indicator by scientists, artists, cinematographers, historians, and designers—and also provide students with a better understanding of their own and other cultures.

ROBERT L. HUMPHREY, JR., Professor Emeritus of Anthropology,
George Washington University, Washington, D.C.

Egypt: Ancient and Modern

Through all of Egypt's many incarnations, the beauty of ancient Egyptian architecture, art, and costume has continued to fascinate and enchant. Today, almost 2,000 years after the fall of ancient Egypt, its great civilization lives on in the minds of anyone who has ever visited this beautiful and complex nation.

Rising from tributaries in the Sudan and Ethiopia, the Nile River flows north to the Mediterranean Sea, through the heartland of Egypt. Originally, the country consisted of two separate peoples—those living in Upper Egypt (to the south) and those living in Lower Egypt (to the north). In about 3100 B.C., these two peoples came together under the rule of King Menes, who created the city of Memphis, in Lower Egypt, as his capital.

There followed a succession of more than 150 monarchs who ruled over ancient Egypt for a period of more than 3,000 years, until the death of Queen Cleopatra VII in 30 B.C. Egypt then fell to a series of foreign rulers. It was part

To this day, ancient Egyptian art, architecture, and clothing continues to inspire modern-day designers. This 18th-century representation of an Egyptian palace shows the grandeur that wealthy Egyptians enjoyed.

of the Roman Empire until A.D. 395, when Byzantium took control. In A.D. 641, it became part of the Arabian empire. The Mamelukes subsequently seized control in 1250, followed by the Ottoman Turks in 1517. Egypt remained under Ottoman control until British occupation in 1881—apart from a brief period when the French held the country under the rule of Emperor Napoleon. Egypt finally became an independent country in 1936.

Dividing Time

Ancient Egypt lasted for such a long time that historians have divided it up into **dynasties**, based on groups of monarchs belonging to 32 particular families. These dynasties are further grouped into six periods: Archaic Period, Old Kingdom, Middle Kingdom, New Kingdom, Late Period, and Greco-Roman Period. There are also three Intermediate Periods, about which we know very little. The most important of these periods are the Old Kingdom (2686–2181 B.C.) and the New Kingdom (1570–1070 B.C.). The kings who built the pyramids at Giza lived during the Old Kingdom, while the New Kingdom saw the first pharaohs, including Tutankhamen (1347–1339 B.C.), whose tomb was discovered in the Valley of the Kings early in the 20th century.

Pyramids are tombs skillfully constructed from blocks of stone, with burial chambers hidden deep inside. It is because of the pyramids that we know so much about how the ancient Egyptians lived. Egyptian tombs were brightly painted with scenes from the life of the deceased. They were also filled with everything that the dead person was believed to need in the afterlife, including clothes, jewelry, weapons, and furniture. During the Archaic Period, these items, known as grave goods, also included servants, who were sacrificed and buried in the tomb so that they might continue serving their masters in the afterlife. By the time of the Old Kingdom, however, this practice had stopped, and statues were used to represent members of the deceased's household.

When **archaeologist** Howard Carter first entered the tomb of the young pharaoh Tutankhamen in 1923, he was astounded by what he saw. Piled high in every corner were priceless objects—a royal throne, gilt beds and footstools, and life-sized statues of the king himself, in a kilt and golden sandals. There was evidence that tomb robbers had been in the chamber, but the ramshackle way that the grave goods were piled up indicated that the thieves had been disturbed. Most of the grave's contents were still there. It was an important find. How people in the past looked and dressed gives historians vital clues about a civilization's culture and beliefs. Finds such as Tutankhamen's tomb give us important insights into the complex world of ancient Egyptian civilization.

Status and Wealth

Tutankhamen, like all pharaohs, was believed to be a living incarnation of Horus, god of the sky, and the son of Ra, god of the sun. In theory, the pharaoh was the most important person in Egypt—at the top of the social ladder. In reality, he shared power with the priests and wealthy landowners.

A selection of headdresses worn by female members of a pharaoh's family. The figure on the right is Queen Nephertari, wife of Rameses II. She wears a vulture headdress, which symbolizes Maati, the goddess of truth.

Blue Hair, Bull's Blood, and False Beards

Egyptian men and women took great care with their appearance. Body hair was considered particularly unsightly, and tweezers and razors found in tombs of the period testify that both men and women removed their unwanted hair. Due to the heat, hair on the head was generally kept short, with both men and women wearing a style similar to a long version of the modern **bob**. Wigs, which became fashionable after 1150 B.C., were often worn, particularly if the wearer was going gray or bald. Egyptians dreaded baldness and applied mixtures containing cat's or bull's blood to their heads in an attempt to keep their locks from thinning. Wigs, when worn, were generally fairly natural-looking, although there is some evidence that they were sometimes dyed in fantastic colors, including blue. Most men were clean-shaven, but long, interwoven beards that protruded from the chin do appear in paintings from the period. Fake beards, made from real hair, were worn for ceremonial occasions by pharaohs, both male and female.

Merchants and craftsmen made up the Egyptian middle class, and farmers comprised the bulk of the lower classes. Slaves, who were generally prisoners of war, were the least important group in Egyptian society. The royal families of ancient Egypt used their power to command the construction of a great many temples, monuments, and statues. These structures had spiritual significance for the Egyptians, as they were designed to please the particular gods that a royal family chose to worship. Such structures were extremely expensive to make, however, because of the time and effort required. The Egyptians solved this problem by capturing people from other nations and keeping them as a slave-labor force. This way, they had a free workforce—all they had to do was keep them fed and watered and provided with the most basic accommodations

A pharaoh and his queen are shown here. As a symbol of his status, the pharaoh wears a crown decorated with a *uraus*, an image of a hooded cobra. His queen wears a crown of Isis, the goddess of healing.

and clothing. Many thousands of captives lived and died in ancient Egypt in this manner.

One Style for All

Despite these clear social divisions, basic Egyptian clothing varied little in appearance from one class to another, although the wealthy could afford garments that were better made and more expensively decorated.

Because of Egypt's hot, dry climate, most Egyptians wore as little as possible. Even the pharaoh, unless dressed for ceremonial occasions, was scantily clad. For men, the most basic garment was a **loincloth**, which was generally the only covering worn by laborers. Richer Egyptians wore the loincloth as an undergarment, and Tutankhamen's tomb contained 100 of these, all neatly folded.

On top of the loincloth was worn a kilt-like skirt, which was either worn knee-length, with a stiff box pleat at the front, or in a longer, more draped style. Women's skirts were generally longer and worn with a belt, the ends of which hung down the front of the skirt. Often, both men and women would leave the upper body bare. By the time of the New Kingdom, a long, pleated, unisex garment called a *kalasiris* was introduced. This was probably made in one piece to give the finished garment an elastic-like quality that made it cling tightly to the wearer's body. The *kalasiris* either covered the entire body from the neck to the ankles, or, for women, finished just below the breasts with shoulder straps to hold it in place.

Rather than cotton or linen cloth, clothes for the wealthy were often cut from colored silk, **brocaded** with silver or gold thread, or embroidered with richly dyed thread. They also wore ornate headdresses, which took a variety of forms. Some were crowns, others were helmets, and both came in many sizes and shapes. The most distinctive headdress can be seen on the image of Tutankhamen, on the Sphinx, and on the other statues of pharaohs. It is a striped crown with side panels that frame the face and extend down the chest. On the forehead of this headdress are mounted crests that show the identity of the wearer.

For Valor

Egyptian soldiers who had displayed particular bravery and daring on the battlefield could expect to be rewarded by being given the Gold of Valor. This was a necklace made from eight ounces (225 g) of solid gold. Hanging from the golden chain were three huge, hand-sized flies. Queen Ahhotep is believed to have won it several times for leading troops into battle on behalf of her son, Ahmose.

Flexible Flax, Golden Jewelry

Flax, from which linen is made, grew in abundance along the banks of the Nile River, and most ancient Egyptian clothing was made from it. Linen is a lightweight and flexible material that can be woven into many forms, from coarse, heavy cloth to a fine, almost see-through material. Egyptians had a fine eye for beauty and liked to contrast the rich tones of

Hair ornamentation was popular in ancient Egypt. The simplest but most elegant of these was a fillet, or ribbon, about two inches (5 cm) wide, worn tied around the head. Often, a lotus blossom (real or fake) was draped across the head, which can be seen in the style shown above.

their naturally dark skin color with bleached white linen. Rich borders, with geometric or symbolic **motifs**, were added for color and contrast. As the upper body was generally left bare, people wore collars made from rows of brightly colored beads or semiprecious stones. As pharaoh, Tutankhamen would also have worn a pectoral, which was a gold and enamel cutout ornament hanging from a gold chain around the neck.

The ancient Egyptians used gold extensively in their chunky armbands, bracelets, and anklets, which were designed to emphasize the shape and length of their limbs. Gold and silver were suitable for making jewelry because they were **malleable** metals and could also be cast into shapes by using a technique known as the **lost-wax process**. Once shaped, the gold or silver could then be set with precious and semiprecious gems or inlayed with glass and **lapis lazuli**. Interestingly, silver was considered more valuable than gold in ancient Egypt because it was more rare in that part of the world. A remarkable characteristic of gold is that it never tarnishes by reacting with other chemicals, which means that ancient Egyptian jewelry remains as bright and shiny as the day it was made, even after thousands of years.

This figure is a member of the royal household, as shown by the addition of the *uraus*, or cobra head, to the headband. The practice of wearing animal skins draped over the shoulder continued through most of the Old Kingdom (2686–2181 B.C.).

Hippo Fat and Makeup

Both men and women in ancient Egypt wore makeup to accentuate the features that were considered most attractive. Kohl—a thick black paste made from ground lead sulphide—was worn around the inside of the eyelids to dazzling effect. Perfume and body oils, made from hippopotamus or crocodile fat, were also used extensively. For formal occasions, women would wear a cone of perfumed wax on the crown of their head, which, as it melted, covered the wig with scent. Perfume was considered to be so vital that craftsmen working on the tombs are recorded to have gone on strike when their expected allowance of this item did not arrive on time.

Fit for a King

Tutankhamen's tomb contains only the best examples of ancient Egyptian craftsmanship: a golden fan decorated by ostrich feathers that the king himself had gathered while hunting; a collection of 130 walking sticks, one "cut with his own hand"; and 100 loincloths. Tutankhamen's wardrobe was expensive, not just because of the gold and gems that it contained, but because of the great amount of time it would have taken to make the king's garments. It has been estimated that just one of the many finely embroidered undershirts in his tomb took 3,000 hours to make. Gloves were so time-consuming to make that only Egypt's wealthiest could afford them. Tutankhamen's tomb contained 27 pairs.

Bulls, Baboons, and Beetles

In the religion of the ancient Egyptians, various gods were responsible for a different component of the world around them. Animals often represented these gods: bulls (which were linked with Montu, the god of war), cats (which represented the goddess Bastet), scarab beetles, vultures, rams, baboons, and jackals. Their gods were real to the Egyptians, and jewelry shaped to represent aspects of the gods was popular. For example, in a society where most people lived by the river and drowning was a real possibility, fish **amulets**—sewn into a type of belt called a girdle or worn around the neck—were given to children to protect them from drowning. Pregnant women would wear amulets carved in the shape of a hippopotamus. This animal represented Taweret, the goddess of fertility, who protected women from harm during childbirth.

By far, the most dangerous time for any Egyptian, however, was after death. Wandering the underworld in search of the Hall of Judgment, the deceased's spirit was in constant danger from evil spirits. Mummies found throughout Egypt have protective blue amulets wrapped within the layers of linen bandages. In addition, the coffins (called sarcophagi) and the walls of the tombs were richly decorated with carvings and paintings depicting the gods, often shown in half-human, half-animal form. Over the heart of the dead person was placed an ornament called a heart scarab. This was

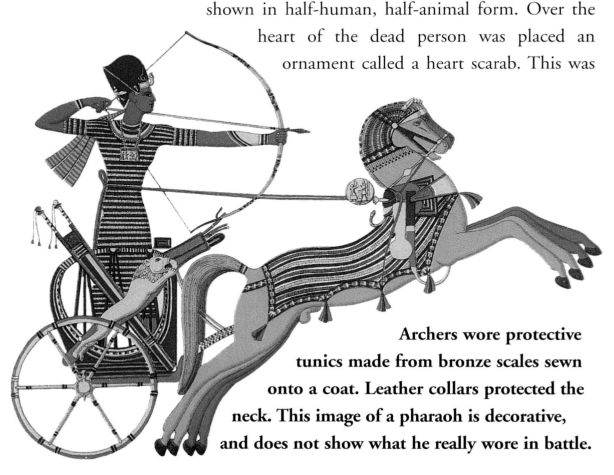

Archers wore protective tunics made from bronze scales sewn onto a coat. Leather collars protected the neck. This image of a pharaoh is decorative, and does not show what he really wore in battle.

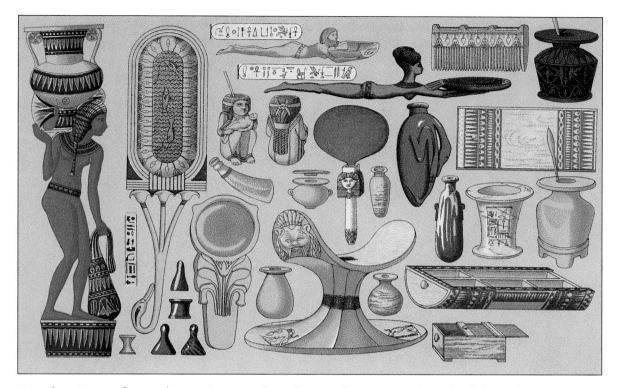

A selection of combs, mirrors, bowls, and jars used to hold makeup: the two items shaped like swimming women, near the top, are cosmetic spoons that were used to mix dyes.

inscribed with prayers from the Egyptian book of the dead, called *The Book of Coming Forth by Day*, which was a guide to reaching the afterlife, telling people what to expect and how to behave.

Egypt Today

Today, Egypt is an Arab country, so the people tend to wear typical Arab clothing. The Egyptians are generally less devout Muslims, however, and have been more heavily influenced by the clothing of other cultures. **Pantaloons** are frequently worn with loose shirts, for example, and headgear is usually a Persian turban or a fez. The Persian turban is a felt cap with a band of twisted fabric around the sides, so that the crown of the cap still shows. The fez is a conical felt hat with a **truncated** or flat peak, sometimes including a decorative tassel.

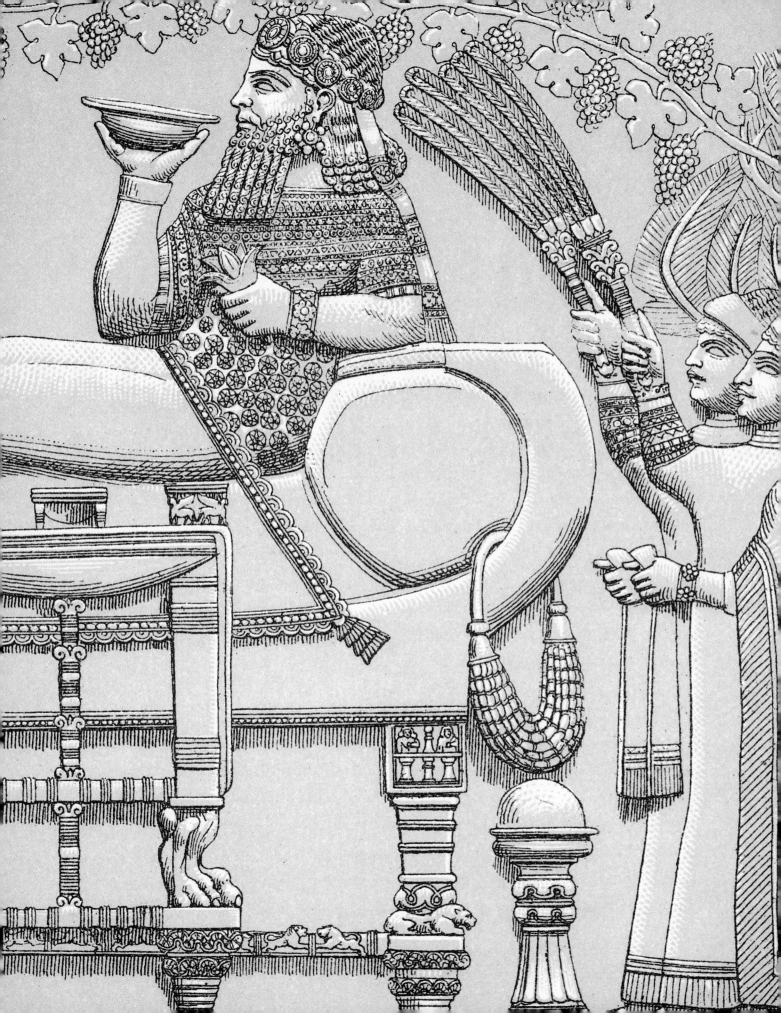

The Assyrian Empire

Famed in the Bible for rising from the Garden of Eden, the Tigris and the Euphrates rivers embrace a strip of land traditionally known as Mesopotamia, where a succession of different peoples has settled over the past 5,500 years.

The Tigris and Euphrates rise in the mountains of modern-day Turkey and flow southeastward for some 800 miles (1,300 km) to the Persian Gulf. Between them lies a fertile plain in a region that is otherwise dominated by mountains and deserts. Mesopotamia is now the heartland of modern-day Iraq. Its capital city, Baghdad, stands where the Tigris and Euphrates almost converge. Historically, this point is where Mesopotamia was divided in two, both culturally and geographically.

Brothers and Rivals

The first cultures to establish themselves in Mesopotamia were the Akkadian, in the north, and the Sumerian, in the south. Sumeria is considered to be the

An Assyrian king relaxes on a couch, attended by female slaves with fans. Note the similarities in dress for both sexes. Women's hairstyles, too, vary little from those worn by men of the period.

world's first civilization, dating from around 3500 to 4000 B.C. By about 2500 B.C., the Assyrian empire was becoming more powerful, having begun in a region surrounding the northern section of the Tigris. The city of Assur (or Ashur), now known as Ash Sharqat, was the empire's first capital. In 668 B.C., following nearly 1,700 years of gradual expansion, the Assyrian empire took a sudden stranglehold on the Middle East region. When the Assyrian emperor Esar-haddon (680–669 B.C.) died, his twin sons, Ashur-bani-pal and Samas-sum-yukin, succeeded him.

Ashur-bani-pal became the king of Assyria (northern Mesopotamia) and Samas-sum-yukin became king of Babylonia (southern Mesopotamia). Ashur-bani-pal was more ambitious than his brother, however, and immediately began to conquer the Egyptians, with whom their father had been at war. By 650 B.C., his armies had taken the entire eastern coast of the Mediterranean and Egypt's Nile Valley. Sensing the threat of invasion, Samas-sum-yukin declared war on his brother, but the Assyrian alliance forces were superior in manpower to the Babylonian armies. In 648 B.C., after two years of fighting, Samas-sum-yukin chose to die within the burning walls of his besieged palace in Babylon rather than suffer the humiliation of capture by his twin.

With Babylonia under his belt, Ashur-bani-pal went on to conquer northern Arabia, thereby including within his empire the whole of what is called the Fertile Crescent. (This stretched from around the Tigris and Euphrates rivers in a semicircle from Israel to the Persian Gulf.) However, by this time, Assyria was in trouble. Finally, in 612 B.C., the new Assyrian capital city, Nineveh, was sacked by a coalition of forces from Medes and Babylon, and the once-great empire was destroyed forever.

Today, a small vestige of the Assyrian empire still survives in the language of some of the many populations scattered over the region. Assyrian is a dialect of Aramaic, a Semitic language spoken by about 200,000 primarily Christian people of northern Iraq. It survived because it was used as a common tongue among the many different peoples who have occupied the region since the

Assyrian art rarely depicts women. Instead, figures of elaborately attired men, often soldiers, stare fiercely out from the relief sculptures— reminders of the might of this once-powerful empire.

demise of the Assyrian empire; including Medians, Persians, Romans, Sassanians, Arabs, Muslims, Abbasids, Tatars, Mongols, and Turks.

Simplicity and Splendor

By 1300 B.C., the Assyrian empire had swallowed up much of western Asia, incorporating many different ethnic groups, including the Philistines and Phoenicians, who we mostly know about from the Old Testament of the Bible. In ancient Egypt, despite clear social divisions, people could and did move up the social ladder—especially skilled craftspeople, whose talents were rewarded handsomely by the pharaoh. In Assyria, most people worked the land, and wealth was tied up in the hands of a few. These **aristocrats** and priests displayed their status in their rich costumes. Wall carvings from the period show Assyrian men covered, almost from head to toe, in gold and gems. Despite this extravagant use of ornamentation, however, the basic Assyrian costume remained quite simple.

Like all cultures of the ancient world, the way that most Assyrians dressed was directly related to their status or occupation. Clothes were expensive to make and difficult to clean, so even the rich wore garments that were designed to be practical and durable. Throughout most of Assyrian history, rich and poor people alike wore a simple, short-sleeved, T-shaped linen **tunic**. This had a high, round-necked collar, and the length varied from knee to ankle, depending on the occupation of the wearer. People who worked in the fields or labored in the cities wore shorter, more practical clothes. However, rich Assyrians also wore a short tunic when hunting. This was generally tied with a brightly decorated, wide leather belt. A loincloth was worn as an undergarment, and sandals protected the feet.

There is little visual evidence to show what Assyrian women wore, because Assyrian art seldom depicted women, apart from female royalty, their ladies-in-waiting, and goddesses. What evidence there is suggests that fashions were fairly unisex, with little difference between male and female costume. The basic T-shaped tunic seems to have been worn equally by Assyrian women,

although they seemed to prefer it longer and with three-quarter-length sleeves. As the Mesopotamian climate was generally warm all year round, little else apart from a tunic was worn during the day. Occasionally, shawls, draped over the left shoulder and gathered under the right arm, were added to complete the costume.

Military Dress Codes

Central to the Assyrian culture was its army. The ancient world required any civilization to be skilled in warfare if it wanted to

Gaudy Garb

Like most people of the ancient world, the Assyrians used linen and occasionally wool for their robes. If wall paintings from the period are to be believed, these robes were almost always bleached white or dyed, as preferred by the Egyptians. Natural vegetable- and animal-based dyes were used to color cloth in a variety of shades, including black, rich greens, vibrant reds, and purples. Gems and golden thread would also be worked into the cloth to create a bright, somewhat gaudy, effect. Similarly, leather would be painted or inlaid with brass or gold decoration, depending on the wealth of the wearer. Tassels and fringes, used to show status, were also used in abundance around hems, on the edges of shawls, and on belts.

An Assyrian king, fourth figure from the left standing under the parasol, is identifiable by his headdress (called a tiara), which, although similar to other headwear of the period, had a point on top.

expand and last for more than a few years. The Assyrian Empire was dominant in the Middle East for about 2,000 years precisely because of its **prowess** in war. Assyrian warriors were divided into regiments according to their fighting specialty. There were foot soldiers (the infantry), those mounted on horseback (the cavalry), and drivers of horse-drawn chariots (the charioteers). As a fighting force, other populations greatly feared the Assyrian armies, because they were ruthless combatants, cutting down anyone who stood in their way.

At the heart of the ancient Assyrian army was the cavalry, whose members wore undershirts and kilts cut from woven linen. These garments offered little practical protection from enemy weapons, but they did allow ease of movement and were cool in the thick of battle. The cavalry wore some protection over their most vulnerable areas, however, such as conical helmets on their heads and breastplates made from beaten sheets of copper or bronze. They also sometimes wore chain mail over their knees or had jointed, armor-plated boots to guard their lower legs from sword blows. Most of their protection came from large oval shields worn on one arm, which could be positioned defensively in combat. The horses, which the men depended on for their lives, were equipped with

Ancient Hair Care

Assyrians had thick, black hair, which they oiled to keep it clean and well conditioned. Both sexes took great pride in growing it long and showing it off as much as possible. The men kept their hair in a style known as a *catagon*, which involved knotting the hair at the rear of the head, then bringing it forward in two tails that fastened over the forehead. Hair was also curled and braided for decoration, including the beard and mustache that most Assyrian men sported. Assyrian women had even more elaborate hairstyles, involving knots on the sides of the head, as well as the rear.

In other ancient civilizations, long garments were evidence of the wearer's wealth. In Assyria, a costume's length varied for purely practical reasons. In this image, a soldier wears short, more practical clothes. The king, under the parasol, wears long ceremonial robes.

armored collars. These protected the vulnerable breast area, where the horse's heart could be pierced with an enemy sword or spear.

Slings and Arrows

Assyrian artillery consisted of infantrymen skilled in the art of firing projectiles at the enemy before going in for hand-to-hand combat. Bronze javelins and spears were thrown from fairly close quarters, while bows and slingshots could be used at some distance. Both arrows and slingshots could be aimed with some accuracy, although javelins and spears usually found their target, too, simply because enemy soldiers would advance in tight formation, thereby offering a larger area to aim at. Due to the relative lack of effective armor available at the time, artillery could and did cut bloody swathes through an enemy force.

Similarly, horse-drawn chariots could also have a devastating effect on the battlefield, functioning in a similar way to armored personnel carriers and tanks in modern warfare. In addition to being useful armored attack-vehicles, chariots could move troops and generals quickly from one point to another during battle. However, the terrain had to be flat and smooth for chariots to operate effectively—which is one of the reasons why battlefields were chosen beforehand in those days. Apart from being a bumpy ride at the best of times, Assyrian chariots were notoriously difficult to control. This was because friction often caused the crude bearings to seize up, making a chariot veer to one side and turn over when traveling at high speed.

Rank and File

Assyrian infantrymen comprised a mix of men from all walks of life. Some were full-time professionals; others were recruited from the fields or towns for

With a good driver dressed in lightweight, practical clothing, chariots could be quite effective in battle, and charioteers were highly regarded members of the Assyrian army.

specific campaigns or were **mercenaries** from other countries. They carried a variety of weapons, such as spears, javelins, swords, daggers, bows, slings, and clubs. Part-time foot soldiers would have been moderately skilled in weapon use, particularly hand-to-hand combat, but those for whom soldiering was a career would have specialized in the use of javelin, sword, bow, or sling. This meant that the whole force could attack in waves, with the least-useful soldiers likely to be killed first. Infantrymen wore knee-length linen tunics, with wide belts for carrying equipment, and leather sandals. For protection, armor comprised a helmet, breastplate, and shield, probably made from beaten bronze sheets. Swords were worn in a wide, leather belt or held in the hand.

Soldiers of high rank, such as generals and royalty, always wore uniforms that reflected their status and wealth. Apart from creating an impression of authority, wearing special uniforms meant that they were easy to identify on the battlefield. Over their tunics, an officer would wear a colorful cloak with a golden helmet and armor adorned with jewels and decorations, so that he could be easily seen with a quick glance from any distance.

Hat Facts

Assyrian priests wore ceremonial robes and headdresses to distinguish them from the masses, as did male and female royalty—although some ceremonies required the participants to perform them naked. Headdresses came in a variety of designs, but they took four basic forms. The most basic was the simple fillet, or headband, which was what the king's attendants usually wore. Non-royals wore truncated and high hats—tall headdresses designed to make the wearer literally stand out in a crowd. Kings and priests generally wore dome-shaped turbans called miters. The tiara was reserved exclusively for use by the king. This tall hat was identifiable by the short, blunt point on its top.

Arabia

At the southeasterly point of the area known as the Middle East, there is a large landmass called the Arabian Peninsula, or simply Arabia. Its inhabitants are sometimes called Arabs, a word first used by the Assyrians to describe a tribe of nomadic people who originally occupied the region that is now modern-day Israel and Jordan.

By 400 B.C., the Arab people had spread all over the area of the Fertile Crescent, across Iraq, Syria, and Palestine. Today, the Arabian Peninsula comprises seven countries: Bahrain (containing 33 islands), Kuwait, Oman, Qatar, United Arab Emirates, Saudi Arabia, and Yemen. Their inhabitants still share a common language and religion.

From Many Gods to One

In the sixth century A.D., the Arabian Peninsula was home to an Arab tribe known as the Qureysh. The Qureysh were Arab nobility grown rich on trade with other nations, especially Syria. The Qureysh are said to have been the descendants of Ishmael, the son of Abraham by his Egyptian slave girl Hagar. Abraham, by his wife Sarah, was also the father of Isaac. Hence, according to the account given in the Bible, Arabs and Jews are both descended from

This image from 1819 shows a selection of tobacco pipes from the Middle and Near East. *Kalians*, also called water pipes, are still used today to smoke tobacco throughout Egypt, Iran, and the Middle East.

Abraham. The Qureysh, like all Arabs, practiced a religion that involved the worship of several gods—a practice known as polytheism—in the form of sacred idols housed within temples. The main temple was the Ka'ba, located in the city of Makkah, or Mecca, which lies in modern-day Saudi Arabia.

In about A.D. 570, a Qureyshi was born who was to change the course of Arab history. He was known as Muhammad. By the time he was six years old, Muhammad had been made an orphan and was subsequently cared for by his grandfather and then his uncle. At the age of 12, Muhammad accompanied his uncle on a trade journey to Syria, where his horizons were widened by contact with other races and religions. During Muhammad's early teenage years, a sacrilegious war ensued between the Qureysh and another Arab tribe, during which Muhammad's character was hardened as a result of witnessing the bloodshed. After this, he took various jobs in and around Makkah to earn his keep, acquiring the title "The Trustworthy"—such was the impression he created in the eyes of others through his competence and honesty.

In A.D. 605, Muhammad started rebuilding the Ka'ba, or temple, which had fallen into a state of disrepair. The tribe quarreled over who should have the privilege of reinstating the sacred Black Stone. Muhammad established his reputation for wisdom by suggesting that a representative from each tribe should hold a corner of the stone during the operation. The four then elevated the stone, which lay on Muhammad's cloak, and carried it into position, ready for insertion into the wall of the Ka'ba. Muhammad used his own hand to push the stone in place, establishing shared honor and peace among the Qureysh.

The Birth of Islam

Shortly after this, Muhammad claimed to have had a divine visitation while praying in a cave near the city of Makkah. The visitation called for Muhammad to restore Abraham's religion—which was based on the belief in just one god, Allah—to the East. Muhammad had a seemingly impossible task ahead of him. It took 10 years for him to convert a band of followers to the new religion he

The Assyrians first used the word *Arab* to describe tribes of nomadic camel herders who traded in and around what is now modern-day Israel and the Jordan. The saddle on this camel features traditional Bedouin weaving.

called Islam. By this time, the Qureysh had begun to see Muhammad as a threat to their traditional faith, and in A.D. 622, Muhammad was forced to flee to Madinah (Medina). The date of his historic flight—the Hijrah—now marks the beginning of the Islamic calendar.

In A.D. 628, following six years of bitter conflict, Muhammad made a peace treaty with the people of Makkah known as the Truce of Al-Hudeybiyah. The truce specified that the Black Stone would became an integral part of the Islamic faith and made Makkah itself Islam's holiest city. Just two years later, Muhammad took Makkah without resistance and made it his capital.

Just as Muhammad changed the faith of Arabia, his successor did the same for the territorial ambitions of the Arab race. Abu Bakr, Muhammad's right-hand man, was elected the first caliph (representative), and he set in motion an era of Islamic conquest that reached its peak during the next century, when the Arabian empire stretched from Constantinople to the Iberian Peninsula of Spain and Portugal.

The Koran, the Islamic holy book, requires all Muslims to pray five times a day—at dawn, noon, mid-afternoon, evening, and night. As this 19th-century illustration shows, during prayer, the head must remain covered.

Today, the Arabian Peninsula is home to a wide range of cultures and traditions, still bonded by the Islamic faith established by Muhammad.

The Legacy of Islam

The traditional garb of Arabia owes much to the climate and terrain of the region. Although Arabians have darkish skin, they are not that well protected from the sun. Therefore, they invented clothes that would cover as much skin as possible, yet allow them to remain cool while they went about their daily lives. In addition to this, the clothing had to protect them from the ravages of sandstorms, which occur frequently in desert areas.

With the rise of Islam, costume took on another role. As is the case in most religions, Islam required its followers to dress with modesty. Islamic writings, such as the Hadith, which are collections of stories and sayings of Muhammad, have many references that tell how Muslims should and should not dress. This quote, from a selection collected by the Islamic scholar Abdul Hamid Siddique, advises Muslim girls who have reached adolescence to cover up their bodies:

"Asma', the daughter of Abu Bakr visited Allah's Messenger...and she had been putting on thin clothes so he (the Prophet) turned away from her and said: 'Asma', when the woman attains the age of puberty, it does not deem proper that her body may be seen except this and this (part of her body) and he pointed to his face and both palms.' (Abu Dawud)"

As a consequence, it became improper for devout Arabian women to expose their bodies to the public gaze.

Modesty and Beauty

Depending on the devoutness of their religious belief, most Arabian women today wear a wide variety of clothing, some showing clear signs of Western influence. However, traditional clothing has remained popular for hundreds of years due not just to the ordinances of Islam, but also to the fact that it is practical and elegant to wear.

The *dara'a* is the name for the full-length, straight-cut underdress that the Arabian woman wears. Over the *dara'a*, a larger, lighter dress is worn, called a *thob* or *thobe*. Beneath the woman's underdress is worn the *sirwal*, a loose-fitting pair of trousers. Over the outer dress is the *abayah*, a full-length cloak-like garment, which is worn hung from either the shoulders or the head. In the past, these garments would probably have have been made from linen, but today, cotton, silk, wool, and manmade fibers are also popular. Generally, the

Enshrouded

In the Muslim holy book, the Koran, Chapter 73 has the strange Arabic title of Al-Muzzammil, which means in English "The Enshrouded One." This odd title is explained in the first verse of this chapter: "O thou wrapped up in thy raiment! Keep vigil the night long…" This refers to a very real and touching event in the Prophet Muhammad's life when he asks his wife Khadîjah to wrap him up in layers of cloaks in preparation for his cold, night-long vigil.

After the 16th century, the Arabian Peninsula became part of the Turkish Ottoman Empire until 1919. These images, from the mid-1800s, show examples of Muslim Ottoman women's dress.

abayah is black, but this is just an outer garment—underneath it, women may be wearing anything from simple, traditional Arabic robes to a brightly embroidered folk dress or the latest designer label.

Faith and Culture

For male Arabians, there is a choice between traditional dress and the Western business suit, although some men wear a combination of the two. For the most part, traditional dress is still popular, not least because it is appropriate for the climate and more comfortable to wear. There is also the influence of the Muslim faith and the desire of Arabs to maintain their own cultural identity.

Like Arabian women, the men wear garments that look like long dresses. These are called *dishdashahs* and are made from silk or cotton. In the summer, *dishdashahs* are usually white, to reflect the sun and keep the wearer cool. In winter, heavier, darker robes are worn. A loose-fitting, sleeved robe called an *aba* is worn over the *dishdashah*. Men also wear loose trousers known as *sirwals*.

One distinctive Arab item of clothing is the traditional headdress, which has three key parts. Placed on the crown of the head is a white cap called the *thagiyah*. Over this is placed a large piece of cloth, folded so that it falls down the sides of the face and around the shoulders. This cloth, called the *gutrah*, is usually white or a white and red plaid. Last, there is the *ogal*, a rope-like hoop that fits around the head to hold the *gutrah* in place. The *ogal*, made from goat hair or sheep wool, is usually black and is twisted to form two or four cables.

The Bedouin Way

The Arabian Peninsula, although large in area, is about 95 percent desert and semi-desert, leaving just 5 percent of the land suitable for farming crops and

Beard Power

The Hadith contains many sayings that relate directly to costume and clothing, as well as to general personal grooming. In hot, dry countries, it is particularly important to keep clean, and many of these sayings have a practical purpose. Some, however, are designed to make a clear distinction between the faithful and the unbeliever. This quote, from a selection collected by the Islamic scholar Abdul Hamid Siddique, encourages Muslims to stand out from those people around them who still believe in many gods (called polytheists) rather than one: "Oppose the polytheists, let the beards grow long and shave the mustaches."

Scarves and Veils

Arabian women wear head coverings, called *chadors*, which are large scarves used to cover the head and shoulders, leaving only the face exposed. An alternative is a lighter, veil-like head scarf called a *shaileh*, which may also be drawn across the face when modesty is required. Other forms of the face veil are the *burgu* and the *yashmak*. The *burgu* covers the nose and mouth, leaving the eyes, cheeks, and chin visible. The *yashmak*, used by devout Arabian women, covers the entire face apart from the eyes, which can be seen through a narrow opening.

livestock, which is the foundation for any settlement and civilization. The Arabian Peninsula was originally one vast territory populated by various Arabic tribes. The area was in a continual state of flux as these tribes vied for supremacy over one another. Today, most of the descendants of these tribes have since settled and adopted semi-Westernized modern lifestyles, but there are still a few tribal populations that roam the area as nomads. Known as the Bedouin, they make their living by taking goods, which they trade across the Arabian deserts in camel trains, and by selling thoroughbred Arabian horses.

Bedouin women are famous for their weaving skills. Even today, many still make their own clothing, cushion coverings, rugs, camel bags, and furnishings, using traditional techniques that have not changed in centuries. The Bedouin use locally available materials, generally sheep or goat wool, to make beautiful garments. These are dyed in a range of colors, from yellow to black, and then embroidered with geometric patterns or designs taken from nature. Tribal motifs or even political slogans are also occasionally used today. Only a few examples of Bedouin weaving skills can be found in museums. This is because, as mentioned, life in the desert can be harsh and there are few resources available, so clothing tends to be worn until it literally falls apart.

Portable Wealth

Bedouin women love jewelry. In Bedouin society, however, jewelry is more than just decoration—it is a symbol of a woman's status. Often, women receive jewelry as wedding gifts and as presents upon the birth of a child. As the Bedouin lifestyle is **nomadic**, jewelry is an easy way of keeping your personal wealth safe and of easily carrying it with you at all times. Arabic jewelry is particularly beautiful. Red and green are seen as lucky colors that can be used to ward off the "evil eye." Because of this, turquoise, coral, and agate are all used in abundance in Arabic jewelry. Bells, too, were traditionally seen as having protective powers, and children's jewelry was often trimmed with tiny bells to ward off evil spirits.

Like clothing, jewelry from the Arabian Peninsula also shows the continuing influence of Islam. The Muslim holy book, the Koran, forbids men from wearing gold, so in Saudi Arabia, wedding rings of silver are worn instead. Islamic designs are used, too, particularly the sign of the hand. As the hand has five fingers, the hand has become a way of representing the Five Pillars (the central beliefs) of the Islamic faith. Following this theme, bracelets and rings are often worn in groups of five. Also popular are exquisitely made cases that hold verses from the Koran. Today, visitors to Arabia return with gifts of Arabic jewelry as reminders of the richness and beauty of Arabia's long history.

House of Hair

One of the largest weaving projects that a Bedouin woman will ever undertake is making the home that she will live in. A traditional Bedouin tent is known as a *bayt al sha'ar*, which means "house of hair." These beautiful brown, black, and white striped tents are made from goat and sheep hair, and they offer excellent protection from the elements, including sandstorms.

Persia and Iran

Geographically, ancient Persia was situated on a plateau surrounded by water to the north and south and mountains to the east and west. This created a naturally fortified region that allowed the Persian empire to survive, more or less unchanged, for over 200 years. Today, Persia is called Iran.

Iran lies between the Persian Gulf and the Indian Ocean to the south and the Caspian Sea to the north. Its western border is shared with Iraq, Turkey, Azerbaijan, and Armenia, while to the east, it borders Pakistan, Afghanistan, and Turkmenistan. Such a location has meant that the people of this region have kept a well-defined identity, despite being included in a number of empires over the past few thousand years.

A Trading Empire

Persia was part of an important overland trade route between Asia and Europe. The Silk Road, as it was known, was used from ancient to medieval times, running from China to the Mediterranean Sea. It covered some 4,000 miles (6,400 km) and ran through the Gobi Desert and over several mountain ranges. The name of the route, the "Silk Road," referred to the large quantities of silk imported across this route to Europe and the Middle East from China. After the late Middle Ages, however, it proved more efficient and profitable to

Shown here are a variety of headdresses for men that were worn throughout the Persian Gulf region during the 18th and 19th centuries.

trade using ships—although Europeans had to sail around Africa to reach the Indian Ocean—because it cut out the middlemen in the Middle East.

Persia means "land of the Aryans." The Aryans first established themselves during the seventh century B.C. in Fars, which was at that time under Assyrian control. Fars lies south of Persia, in the Zagros Mountains, along the coast of the Persian Gulf. In 550 B.C., the Persians, under the leadership of King Cyrus the Great, finally struck out to create their own empire. For 20 years, until Cyrus' death, the Persian empire engulfed Asia Minor, Babylonia, Syria, Palestine, and a good deal of the Iranian **Plateau**.

Cambyses, son of Cyrus, then went on to conquer Egypt in 525 B.C. Darius I—known as "The Great"—took the throne in 521 B.C. and continued

The main element of Persian costume was a simple tunic, with or without sleeves, gathered in with one or more belts. They came in a variety of lengths, as did the coats worn over the top.

Patchwork Clothing

Ancient Persian clothing was made from animal hides. This caused early tailors many problems, because no two hides were the same size, and they were rarely long or wide enough to make one complete garment. Early Persian trousers and coats, then, were made from a patchwork of tanned hides, which were time-consuming and costly to make. Not surprisingly, by 700 B.C., leather was replaced by more flexible, durable materials, such as wool and linen.

where Cambyses had left off. He took the Persian empire westward into Europe and eastward as far as India and the Aral Sea. Darius introduced a system of administration to cope with his enormous empire, but things began to go awry following his death because of feuding within the various dynasties, or ruling families. Finally, between 499 and 449 B.C., Persia was involved in a series of wars with Greece that led to the ultimate decline of the Persian empire. Persia finally fell to the armies of Alexander the Great in 330 B.C.

Sculptures and Paintings

At its height, the Persian empire was a powerful force in the ancient world. Culturally, they borrowed much, blending the traditions of conquered peoples with those of the nomadic tribes in the region. This blending of traditions resulted in a uniquely Persian culture, which can be seen most clearly in the costumes and clothing of its people.

Probably due to the influence of the nomadic tribes, Persian clothing for men was designed to be worn on the move, especially on horseback. Ancient Persians wore a garment virtually unknown in much of the ancient world—trousers. Cut at knee- or ankle-length, these were both simple and practical garments that neatly fitted the legs like modern-day tights. The upper part of

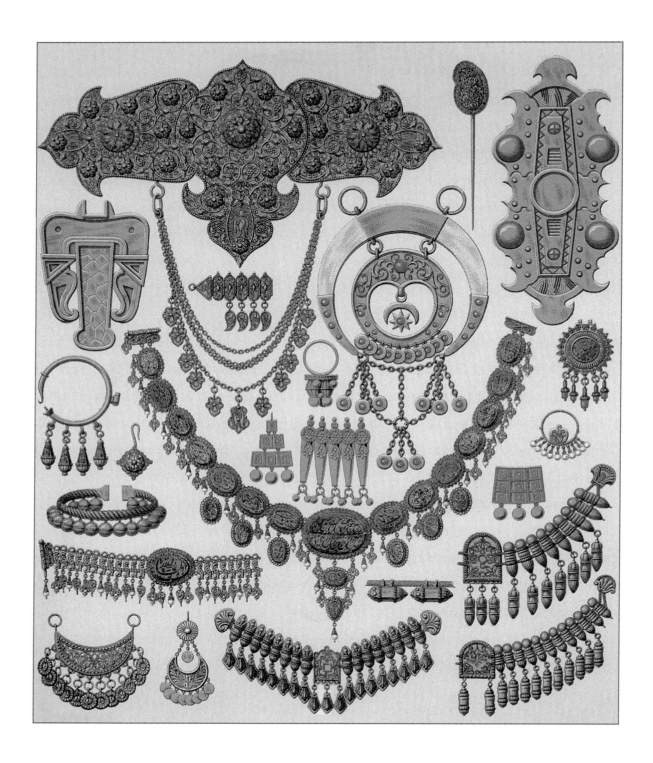

A rich selection of gold and silver Persian jewelry is shown here in an illustration from the early 19th century. Bulky gold chains were worn around the neck by richer women, as were heavy, decorated collars.

the body was covered by a knee-length sleeved coat, which was fastened at the waist with a belt. Hoods were worn on the head, especially in battle or when hunting. These covered the chin and had a peak, which often fell toward the back of the head.

Longer and Wider

Persian dress for women, as in much of the ancient world, tended to be similar to the styles worn by men. The main differences were in the length of the garment. For Persian women, coats were typically worn longer and with a much fuller cut than the men's. They also tended to be sewn up the front, while the men's garment was left open and worn belted.

Unlike the Assyrians, women of ancient Persia wore little jewelry. Statues and paintings from the period show that earrings were popular with men and were probably worn by women, too. Generally, women are portrayed barefoot, although it is likely that both men and women would have worn soft-soled, slipper-style shoes when necessity required it.

Desert and Winds

The region that was Persia, now Iran, is a Muslim country, having become part of the Arabian empire in A.D. 637, when the Arabs captured its capital, Ctesiphon.

High Hats

The Persians were a handsome people who took great care in their costume and grooming. Hair for men and women was worn curled, neatly trimmed, and generally less obviously styled than the Assyrians. Usually, the head was bare, however, one particular style of headdress seemed to have been reserved specifically for the king. This spectacular headdress was a type of crown almost eight inches (20 cm) tall, which flared out from the head so that it was wider at the top than at the bottom.

In architecture, as in folk costume, Persians often used geometric shapes and designs taken from nature, such as flowers or leaf patterns, for decoration on walls, carpet, and the hems of clothing. This is, in part, because Islam forbids the depiction of people or animals.

Geographically, Persia is a country of semi-desert and mountains, with villages, towns, and cities wherever sources of water happen to be. The central Iranian Plateau is subjected to extremes of temperature from day to night and from summer to winter, making it hard work to earn a living. Added to this, sandstorms frequent the area, and they can be so harsh that they kill livestock and humans alike. These are known as the "poison winds." Today, people protect themselves by wearing wraparound scarves called *shamals*. These cover the head to leave only the eyes peering out through a narrow slit. Other long, flowing, Arab-style garments are also worn for protection from the extremes of the weather.

Music and Dance

There is a long tradition of wandering musicians and dancers in the Iranian Peninsula. The musicians are usually male and the dancers female. It is their job to entertain, so they wear costumes that attract the eye during their performance. Iranian music and song have a hypnotic effect on the listener, and the movement of dance adds to the emotive effect. Dancers also wear costume jewelry designed to rattle and glimmer so that it, too, adds to the overall effect. Good troupes of performers are highly respected for their craft and can earn a reasonable living on their travels. This is despite the fact that wealthy Iranians consider dancing a degrading and undignified activity among their own class.

Professional dancers have to be highly skilled and extremely fit because of the energetic way that the body must move during a typical performance. Dances based on those performed in the Middle East (which are slightly different from those performed in Iran) are now becoming popular in the West. "Belly dancing," so-called because of the way the performer rolls her abdomen during the dance, has become a popular form of exercise, and authentic examples of the bright, flowing costumes worn are sought after.

Covering Up

During the rule of the Ayatollah Khomeini (1979–1989), a new constitution based on a strict interpretation of Islamic teachings came into being. This "Islamic revival" resulted in many women choosing to cover their bodies entirely, wearing a long, flowing body veil called a *chador*. However, although Iran is a Muslim country, many people still choose to wear Western clothing.

Iranian men tend to wear loose-fitting garments, such as shirts and pantaloons, over which is worn a robe or cloak when the weather demands it.

They often wear felt hats with truncated peaks, similar to the fez, but taller. Turbans are also a popular choice of headgear and come in a variety of styles. Boys wear bowl-shaped silk caps. Nomadic peoples tend to wear clothing of a more basic nature, with men and women wearing kilts because they afford more freedom of movement in the hot climate. It is common for the lower legs to be bound and for slip-on shoes to be worn.

Egyptians, Persians, or Indians?

Persia was the first Middle Eastern land to be visited by bands of Gypsies, some 800 years ago. Gypsies got their name because Europeans believed that they came from Egypt. However, it is likely that Gypsies came from India around

Persian dancers dressed in bright, flowing costumes that let them move freely during the dance. Their clothes were also designed to stimulate the eye during the performance.

Costly Carpets

Persia is famed for its carpets, called *kilims*. These skillfully woven rugs are made from cotton, wool, or silk. The threads are dyed with a variety of vibrant colors and woven to create beautiful, intricate patterns. The best Persian carpets are those with the finest detail and brightest colors; they represent the greatest amount of time and effort on the part of the craftsman, and sell for considerable prices. Although they are intended to be floor coverings, many Persian carpets are so prized that they are hung on walls to preserve them. The age of a Persian carpet also has a bearing on its value, not least because an old carpet in good condition is rare and difficult to replace.

The turban is a popular style of Middle Eastern headdress. The word *turban* comes from a Persian word, *duldand*, which referred to any type of scarf or length of material that was wrapped around the man's head.

Ancient Persian shoes, when worn, would sometimes curl up at the toes. This style remained popular throughout the Middle East for many centuries, as these images from the 19th century illustrate.

A.D. 1000 and slowly spread across western Asia and Europe. Gypsies speak a language called Romany, which is related to Hindi, thus revealing their ancestral roots. Because Gypsies have no permanent home, they make a living by seasonal work, trade, fortune telling, and putting on shows of dance and folk music.

Traditional Gypsy dress is highly flamboyant and colorful, especially among women. They wear puffed skirts and turban-like hats to ensure that they stand out in the crowd. Despite centuries of persecution, Gypsies still retain their unique culture and costume. Even today, Gypsy clothing is so admired by Europeans that when modern fashion designers talk about Gypsy style, they are referring to the beautiful and colorful flowing clothes that Gypsies wear.

Israel

The country of Israel, which lies on the southeastern shores of the Mediterranean Sea, has a long history, punctuated by war and invasion. At the time of the Old Testament, the region was called Palestine and the people were known as Hebrews.

Hebrews claimed descent from Abraham—as did the early Muslims—who is believed to have come from the city of Ur in Mesopotamia in about 2000 B.C. Over the next few hundred years, the ancient Egyptians held many Hebrews captive and used them as slave labor. In around 1225 B.C., the prophet Moses led the Hebrew slaves—known as the Israelites—from Egypt to Palestine. That 40-year journey is called the Exodus. In the Bible, Moses described Palestine as "the Promised Land" because God had promised the land to His people forever.

The Promised Land

After crossing the Jordan River into the Promised Land, the Israelites attacked Jericho, a Canaanite city, and occupied the region. Having established themselves, the Israelites would have to fight hard to keep their new home.

In 586 B.C., the region was invaded and conquered by the Babylonians under Nebuchadnezzer II. The Israelites were exiled and put to work as slaves once again. Many eventually returned to Palestine—almost 50 years later—in

Costume has always been used to display the status and wealth of the wearer. This ancient Hebrew king, with richly embroidered clothes and costly jewels, enjoys all the trappings afforded by his social position.

539 B.C., when the Persians, led by Cyrus the Great, attacked the Babylonian empire and captured Babylon. The Hebrews faired well under Persian rule, but the **status quo** was brought to a end when Alexander the Great conquered the entire region in 333 B.C. An uprising, known as the Maccabean Revolt, initiated by the Hebrew leader Judas Maccabaeus, led to Jewish independence from 142 B.C. until Palestine fell into the hands of the Roman Empire in 63 B.C.

Roman rule prompted the birth of the Zealot sect, which wanted a Hebrew **theocracy**, basing itself on the idea of a world governed by rabbis (Hebrew clerics), modeled on Palestine between the time of Moses and King Saul. The Zealot Rebellion that ensued resulted in the destruction of Jerusalem in A.D. 70 and the dispersion of the Hebrews, or Jews as they were then called, throughout the Old World. For almost 2,000 years, Palestine was subjected to a series of invasions, resulting in it coming under British protection in 1918.

It was not until 1946 that the independent state of Israel came into being. By that time, Germany's Adolf Hitler and his political party, the Nazis, had murdered more than six million European Jews in a horrific example of prejudice. Between 1941 and 1945, the greater part of Europe's Jews and some other groups were murdered in "death camps" at Hitler's instruction. This genocide was described by Hitler as "the final solution." It has now became known as the Holocaust, meaning "burnt whole" in Greek.

Race and Religion

Throughout much of their history, the Hebrew people have kept themselves apart from the Arab peoples of the Middle East. The main reason for this was their faith. While many ancient civilizations believed in many gods, the Hebrews believed in one. This belief bound the 12 Israelite tribes together and formed the basis for Jewish culture and traditions. Today, the word *Jew* is used to describe both people who follow the Jewish religion and those who may not be religious, but who have a Jewish cultural heritage. Today, Jewish communities are found throughout the world, not just in the Promised Land.

The ancient Hebrews spent several hundred years captive in Egypt. This image, based on a tomb painting, shows ancient Egyptians taking prisoners during battle. Prisoners of war were used as slave labor.

In ancient times, however, Jewish communities were less widespread and would have been identifiable to others by their style of dress.

Poor Men and Prophets

For their clothing, Hebrews relied on sheep and goat wool, which was woven into a simple, short-sleeved, ankle-length tunic. In early periods, poor people would probably have worn just a loincloth or animal skins. Prophets and holy men also wore animal skins as a sign of their **piety**. When King Ahaziah of Israel heard of a man "wearing a cloak made of animal skins, tied with a leather belt" (2 Kings 1:8), he knew that the man described was the prophet Elijah.

Later, it was common to wear two tunics, one of wool and one of linen, one on top of the other. Making clothes involved a huge investment of time, and the poor would wear clothes until they were threadbare. In the story of Joseph in Genesis, his father Jacob, believing him to be dead, tears his clothes in despair. To destroy good clothing was a sign of real grief. Jacob then wore a

As in many cultures, ancient Hebrew religious leaders could be distinguished by their costume. A Pharisee wore a domed turban, and a high priest wore a miter—two versions of which are shown.

The Coat of Many Colors

While the Hebrews may have driven the Canaanite people from the Promised Land, they were happy to adopt many elements of Canaanite costume. The Canaanites were particularly known for their cloth, which they wove into wide, colorful stripes. In the book of Genesis in the Old Testament, Joseph, whose family lived in Canaan, is given a gift of a "long robe with full sleeves" by his father Jacob (Genesis 37:3). This famous "coat of many colors" was probably made in the Canaanite style.

tunic of sackcloth, a coarse cloth made from camel hair and worn by people in mourning. Wearing an outfit made from camel hair would be uncomfortable. Holy men also wore sackcloth as a sign of their devotion to God.

Queens and Harlots

In later periods, Hebrew women were well covered. Simple, long, loose tunics were worn unbelted. These hid the body's natural shape and helped to identify respectable women from the more seductively clothed prostitutes. By the time of the Old Testament, these tunics had become even more voluminous. All respectable women also covered their heads, and while at prayer, they wore a veil that completely hid the face, thus adding to their anonymity.

The Jewish scriptures preached restraint. Jewish women did wear silk, but they preferred linen and wool. Silk was seen as the material of foreign rulers; in the Book of Ezekiel in the Old Testament, the Jewish city of Jerusalem is compared to a prostitute for adopting the trappings of a foreign ruler. In another chapter, the God of the Jews describes how he had strived to make Jerusalem beautiful, giving her all the trappings of a wealthy Hebrew queen:

"I rubbed olive oil on your skin. I dressed you in embroidered gowns and gave you shoes of the best leather, a linen headband...I put jewels on you—bracelets and necklaces. I gave you a nosering and earrings and a beautiful crown to wear. Your beauty was dazzling" (Ezekiel 16:9–12).

Modern Dress

Having been dispersed worldwide, Jews have assimilated themselves into a variety of host cultures over the years. This has led to their adopting or being influenced by the dress of other nations. Modern Jews do not have a traditional dress, but Jews pride themselves on dressing stylishly, with men wearing suits and women wearing dresses or blouses and skirts. Head coverings have remained popular in Jewish populations the world over. Depending on their home, Jewish men have adopted the fez, the **homburg**, or the turban, as well as other kinds of hats. Jewish women have a tradition of wearing head scarves, sometimes wrapped over pillbox hats, or wrapped around caps like a turban.

Being Kosher

Jewish people, particularly Orthodox Jews, follow strict guidelines about the way they live their lives, which are outlined in the Jewish scriptures. The best known are the **kosher** rules, which state what food devout Jews can eat. Acceptable food is termed "kosher," from the Hebrew word for "proper." These rules probably originated for reasons of hygiene and economy, but were incorporated into the Jewish faith to ensure that people followed them.

The Jewish holy book, the Torah, also outlines rules on clothing. These rules, called *shatnez*, forbid Jews to mix linen and wool. Separate garments of wool and linen can be worn together, but clothing that contains both fibers is strictly prohibited. Few people follow these rules today, but those who do have to avoid all clothes that are unlabeled, recycled, or embroidered. People who follow the *shatnez* laws take them seriously, and it has been said that

Nose Rings and Ankle Bracelets

The ancient Hebrews were not as skillful at making jewelry as their Egyptian neighbors, but they nevertheless enjoyed wearing bracelets, necklaces, and rings. Generally, only Hebrew women wore jewelry, but they often wore it in abundance. Rings were even worn through the nose. This love of jewelry was condemned in the Book of Isaiah, which outlined the punishment for vain women: "Look how proud the women of Jerusalem are! They walk with their noses in the air. They are always flirting. They take dainty little steps, and the bracelets on their ankles jingle. But I will punish them—I will shave their heads and leave them bald" (Isaiah 3:16–18).

This ancient Hebrew high priest is dressed in his ceremonial robes. The square pocket on the front of the garment is the "Breastplate of Judgment."

"anyone who is careful to avoid wearing *shatnez* will merit to be dressed in garments of salvation and a cloak of righteousness."

The Letter of the Law

In addition to *shatnez* laws, Orthodox Jews and Hebrew scholars are also required to wear a skullcap called a *yarmulkah*. A *yarmulkah* is an embroidered skullcap worn by Orthodox Jews in public, and by the less devout while at prayer. The Orthodox Jew changes his skullcap for prayer, wearing a plain version called a *kipa* (also spelled *kippa*, *kipah*, or *kippah*).

An Orthodox Jew also wears a fringed prayer shawl called a *tallit* and small leather boxes held against his forehead and wrists with leather bindings. These are called *phylacteries*, and they contain **vellum** parchment bearing Hebrew inscriptions from the Old Testament as a reminder of his commitments at morning prayer. An Orthodox Jewish man also wears side locks, or curls, in imitation of his Hebrew forefathers, thus linking him to the rich traditions of the past.

Glossary

Note: Specialized words relating to clothing are explained within the text, but those that appear more than once are listed below for easy reference.

Amulet a charm often inscribed with a magic incantation or symbol to protect the wearer against evil

Archaeologist a person who studies material remains (such as fossil relics, artifacts, and monuments) of past human life and activities

Aristocrat a person who belongs to the nobility or the upper class

Bob a short haircut

Brocade (v.) to create raised patterns on fabric

Dynasty a succession of rulers of the same line of descent

Homburg a man's felt hat with a stiff curled brim and a high crown creased lengthwise

Kosher sanctioned by Jewish law

Lapis lazuli a semiprecious stone that is usually a rich azure blue color

Loincloth a cloth worn about the waist and hips, often as the sole article of clothing in warm climates

Lost-wax process the use of wax to create a mold for casting bronze

Malleable capable of being extended or shaped by beating with a hammer or by the pressure of rollers

Mercenary a soldier who is hired to fight, usually in a foreign army

Motif a theme

Nomadic relating to people who have no permanent residence, but move from place to place, usually seasonally and within a well-defined territory

Pantaloons loose-fitting trousers that are usually shorter than ankle-length

Pharisee a member of a Jewish sect noted for strict observance of rites and ceremonies of the written law and for insistence on the validity of his own oral traditions concerning the law

Piety devoutness

Plateau a land area having a relatively level surface, raised sharply above adjacent land on at least one side

Prowess skill

Status quo the existing state of affairs

Theocracy government of a state by immediate divine guidance or by officials who are regarded as divinely guided

Truncated cut short; lacking an expected or normal element

Tunic a simple slip-on garment made with or without sleeves and usually knee-length or longer, belted at the waist

Vellum a fine-grained unsplit lambskin, kidskin, or calfskin, prepared especially for writing on or for binding books

Timeline

(B.C. DATES)

3100	Upper and Lower Egypt combine under King Menes.
2500	The Assyrian empire is established.
1125	Moses leads the Israelites on their Exodus from Egypt to Palestine.
11th century	The kingdoms of Israel and Judah are established in Palestine.
7th century	Persian civilization begins in Fars.
668	The Assyrian empire begins its expansion.
612	The Assyrian empire is ended by Mendes and the Babylonians.
586–539	The period of the Babylonian captivity of the Hebrews (Jews).
550	The Persians begin to expand their empire.
539–333	Persian occupation of Palestine.
525	King Cambyses of Persia conquers Egypt.
499–449	The Persian Wars are fought against Greece.
333–331	Macedonian occupation of Palestine.
331–142	Syrian occupation of Palestine.

330	Persian empire ends.
63–A.D. 395	Roman occupation of Palestine.
30–A.D. 395	Egypt is under Roman rule.
5	Jesus of Nazareth is born.

(A.D. DATES)

395–641	Byzantine occupation of Palestine; Egypt is under Byzantine rule.
570	Muhammad is born in Mecca, Arabia.
632-633	Muhammad dies; the Arab Muslim empire begins expansion.
637–1099	Arab Muslim occupation of Palestine.
641–1250	Egypt is part of Arab Muslim empire.
1099–1199	The First Crusade establishes Palestine as part of Christendom.
1517–1918	Ottoman occupation of Palestine.
1500s	The Arabian Peninsula falls to the Ottoman Empire.
1801–1936	Ottoman, then British, occupation of Egypt.
1914–1918	World War I.
1918–1947	British stewardship of Palestine.
1919	The Arabian interior is freed from Ottoman rule.
1932	Mesopotamia becomes Iraq; Saudi Arabia emerges from former Arabia.
1935–1936	Persia becomes Iran; Egypt is proclaimed an independent state.
1939–1945	World War II; Holocaust under the Nazis in Europe.
1943–1946	Lebanon and Syria become independent.
1947	The United Nations votes for the partition of Palestine.
1948	The independent state of Israel is proclaimed.
1951–1961	Oman and Kuwait emerge from former Arabia.
1970–1972	Yemen, Qatar, and United Arab Emirates emerge from former Arabia.

Online Sources

Arab Heritage Information
www.arab-heritage.com
A Web site about the culture, customs, language, and crafts of the Arab people, for information specifically about costume, click on "clothing."

The Costumer's Manifesto
www.costumes.org
An extensive Web site featuring information about world costume and hundreds of links to other good sites.

"The Original Arab, The Bedouin"
www.webstories.co.nz/focus/deserts/hittmai1.
html
An extract from the book *The Arabs: A Short History*, by Philip K. Hitti (1996).

The Palestinian Heritage Foundation
www.cafearabica.com/issue1/sections/culture/
cultright.html
A historical glimpse on Palestinian couture and the Middle Eastern textile industry, with picture gallery.

Further Reading

Fleming, Fergus and Alan Lothian. *The Way to Eternity: Egyptian Myth*. London: Duncan Baird, 1997.

Harris, Nathaniel. *Hamlyn History of Ancient Egypt*. London: Hamlyn, 1997.

Hourani, Albert (Advisory Ed.) and Trevor Mostyn (Exec. Ed.) *Cambridge Encyclopaedia of the Middle East and North Africa*. Cambridge: Cambridge University Press, 1988.

Keene, Michael. *Examining Four Religions*. London: Harper Collins, 1997.

Schulz, Regine (ed.) *Egypt: Land of the Pharaohs*. New York: Konemann, 2002.

Siddiqui, Abdul Hamid. *Selection from Hadith*. Safat, Kuwait: Islamic Book Publishers, 1993.

Zuhur, Sherifa (ed.). *Images of Enchantment: Visual and Performing Arts of the Middle East*. Cairo, Egypt: Amer University in Cairo Press, 2001.

About the Authors

Gerard Cheshire is a graduate of the University College London in Physical, Cultural, and Social Anthropology (BSc Hons). He has written on a variety of reference topics, many of which relate to anthropology. They include the history of science and technology, human evolution and design, and the history of civilizations and warfare. Gerard regards this project as an interesting and worthwhile assignment because his philosophy is that the more we understand the world around us and our own past, the better able we will be to understand and deal with the complexities of modern life.

Paula Hammond was born and educated in the ancient Roman town of Chester, England. After completing a degree in History, Literature, and Theology at Trinity College, she moved to London to pursue a career in publishing. Her writing credits include *Communication Through The Ages*, which traces the history of writing and communication, and *The Grubbiest Adventure...Ever*, a project-based research resource for young children. She is currently writing a series for teenagers on notable historical figures and events.

Index